GEOLOGY FOR KIDS PICTIONARY

GEOLOGY ENCYCLOPEDIA OF TERMS CHILDREN'S ROCK & MINERAL BOOKS

BABY PROFESSOR
EDUCATION KIDS

Speedy Publishing LLC
40 E. Main St. #1156
Newark, DE 19711
www.speedypublishing.com
Copyright 2017

All Rights reserved. No part of this book may be reproduced or used in any way or form or by any means whether electronic or mechanical, this means that you cannot record or photocopy any material ideas or tips that are provided in this book.

In this book, we're going to talk about geology terms. So, let's get right to it!

Geology is a field of study that includes all the matter that's part of the Earth. Scientists who specialize in the field of geology are known as geologists. They study the materials that compose the Earth, such as rocks and minerals, and the forces that shape the Earth, such as earthquakes and volcanic eruptions.

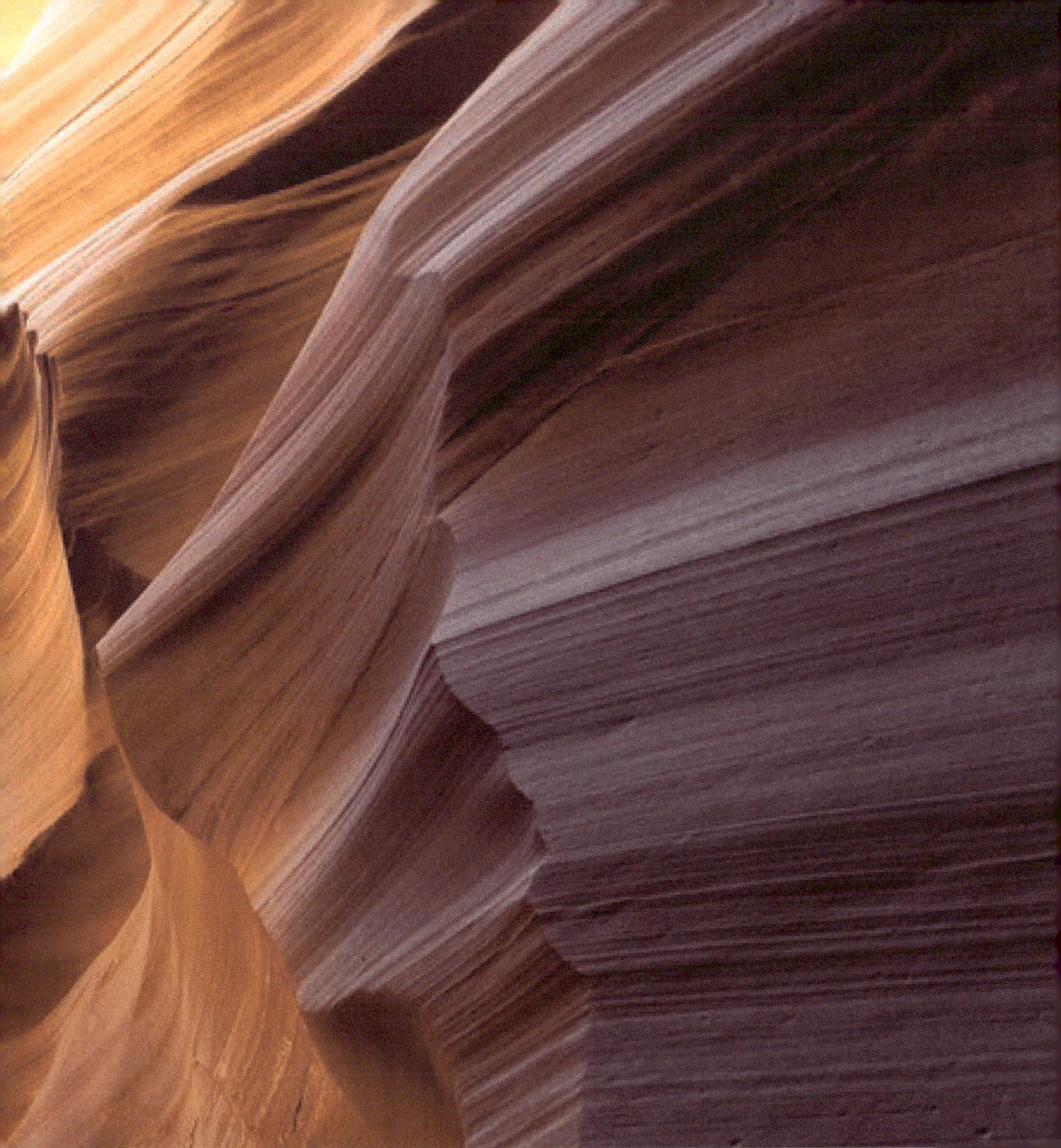

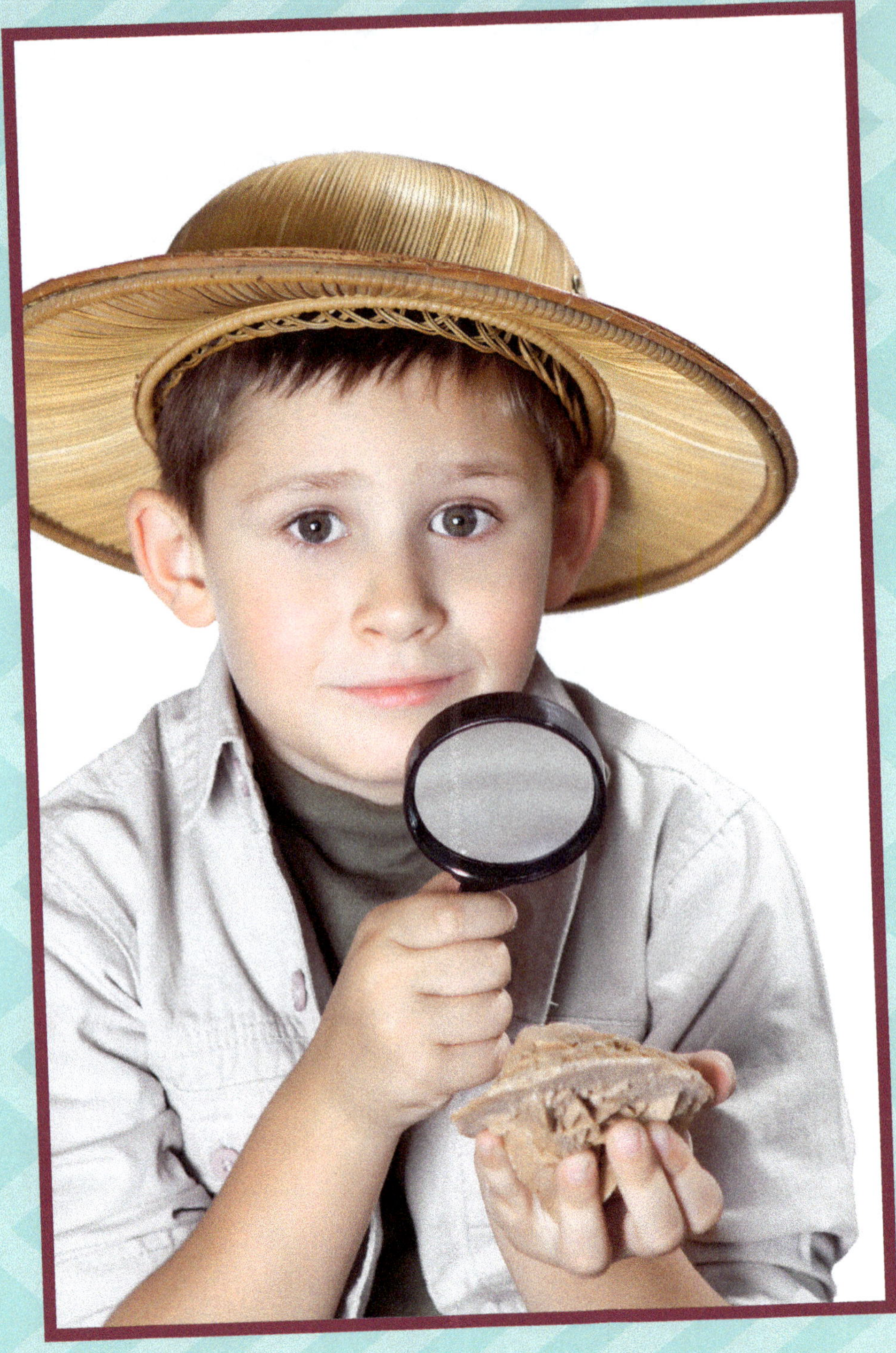

Land formation, fossil records, and climate change are important areas of geology research. Geologists study the Earth's past so they can make informed recommendations about future decisions that impact the Earth.

ABLATION: The melting of ice and snow from the surface of a glacier due to evaporation from a change in the temperature or erosion by winds

AEOLIAN PROCESS: A change in the Earth's surface, such as sand dunes, caused by the activity of wind

AGE: A time span that lasts for several million years and that is shorter than the time span designated by an epoch

AMBER: A resin that comes from a cone-bearing tree and sometimes contains fossilized insects

AQUIFER: A natural formation of rock that is permeable and that holds and transmits groundwater

ARCHIPELAGO: A collection of islands

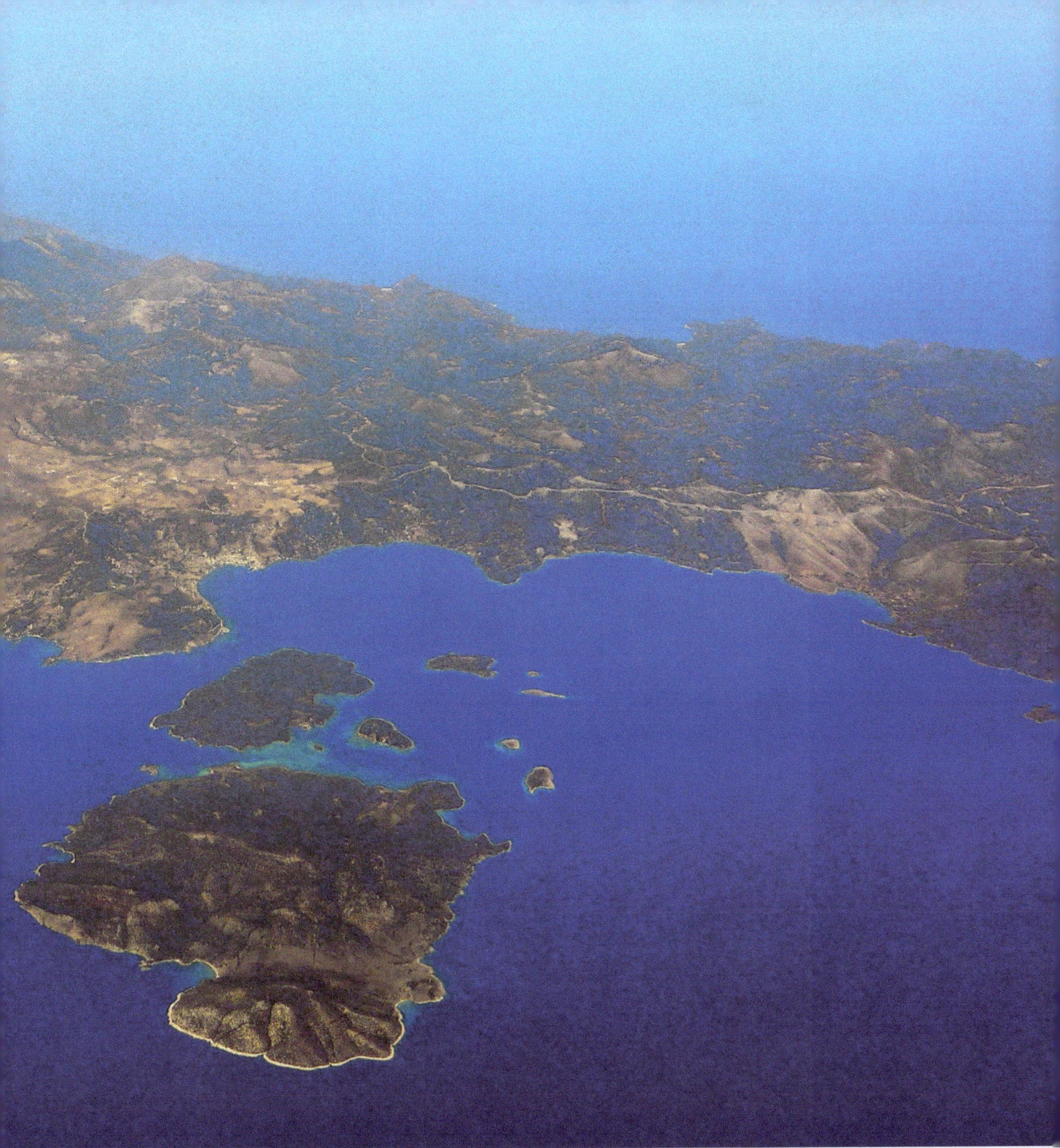

ASH: Very fine grey dust that is formed when a volcano erupts

ATOLL: A broken or continuous circle of coral islands and reef located around a lagoon

BARRIER ISLAND: An elongated island that is located parallel to the shoreline

BASALT: A type of igneous rock that is fine-grained

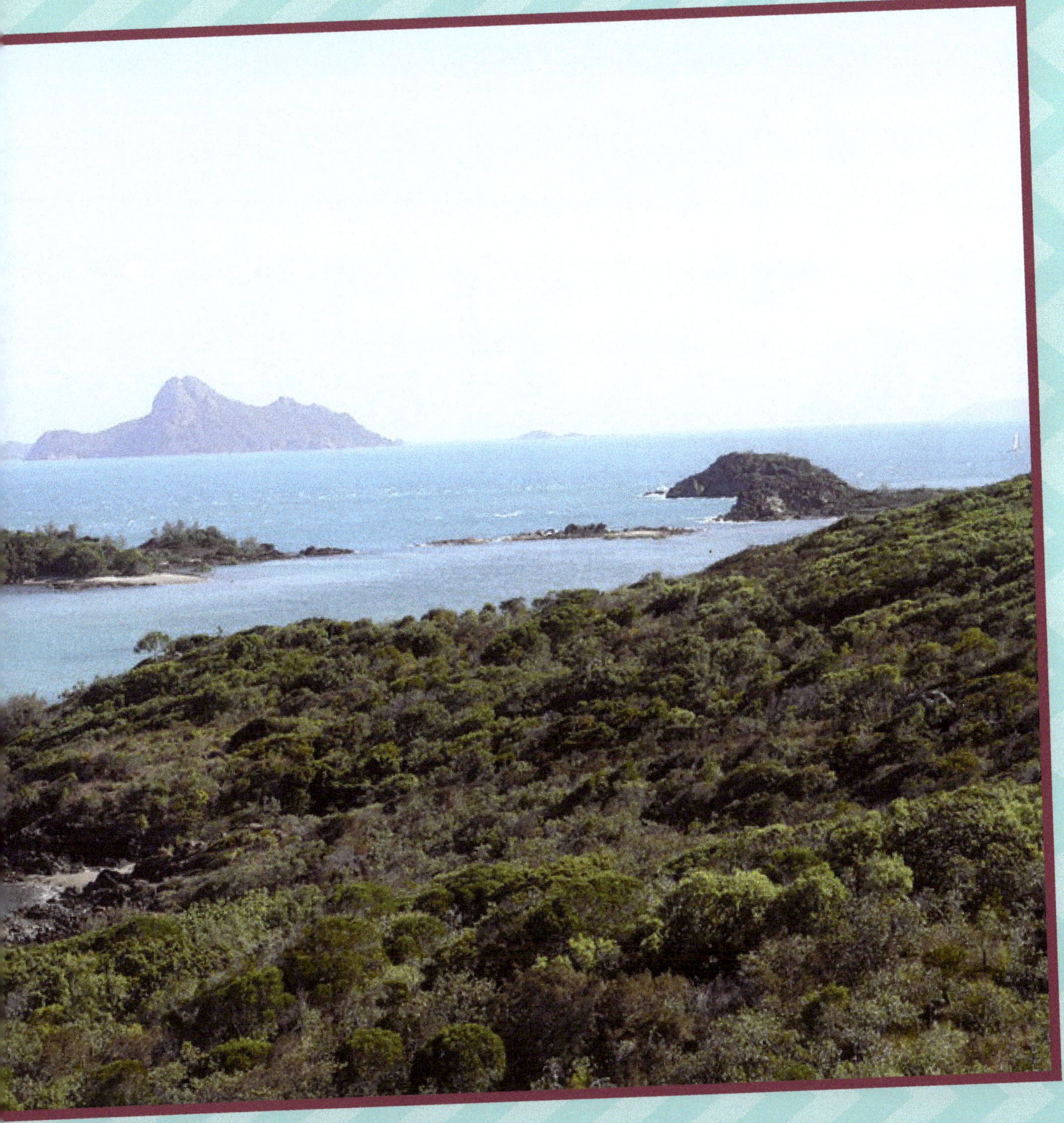

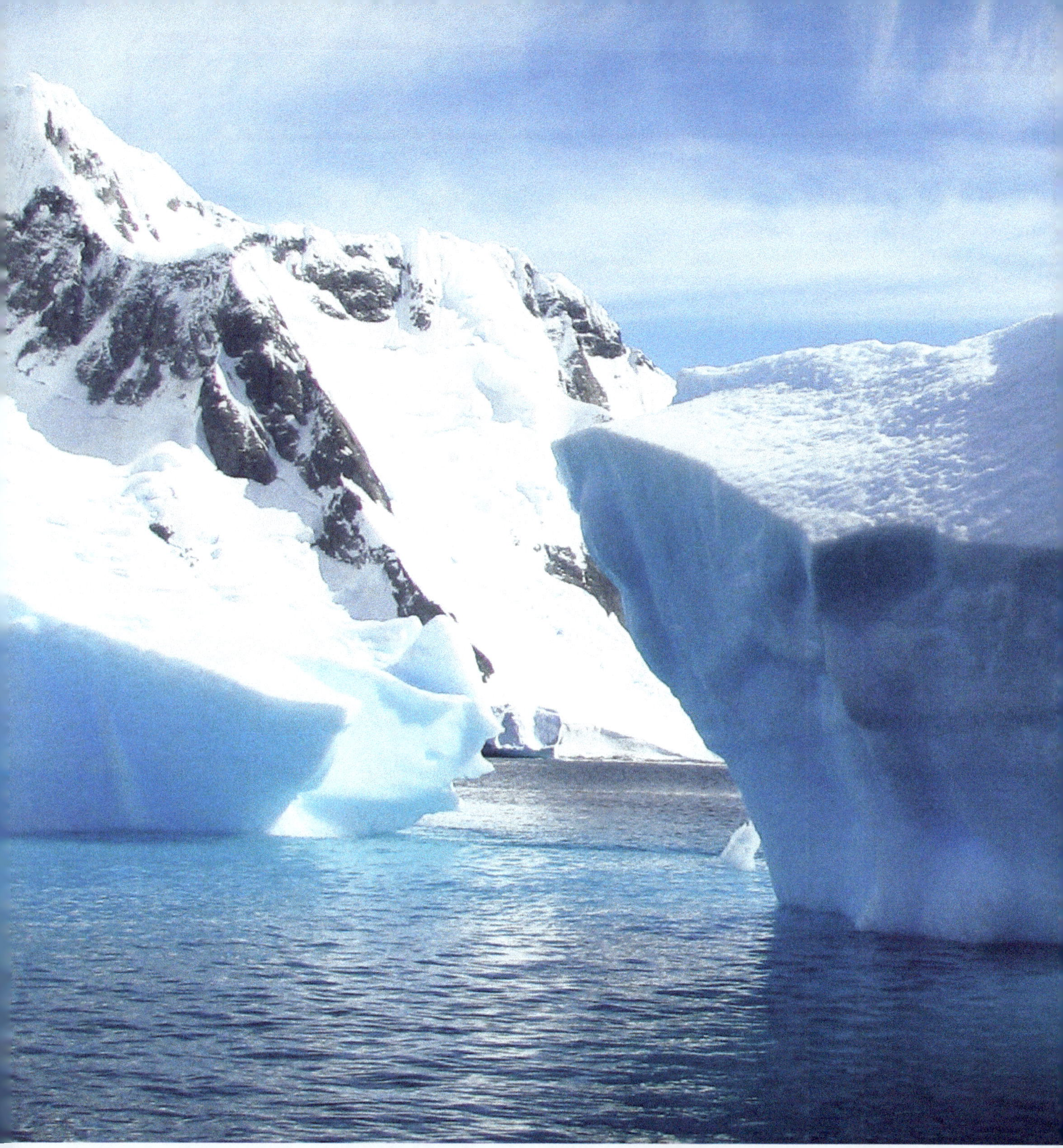

BEDROCK: The layer under the loose soil surface that is composed of solid rock

BERG: A floating or stationary section of ice

BUTTE: A hill with a flat top and steep sides with a summit area that isn't as large as a mesa

CALDERA: A large depression in the Earth that is circular and is formed by either the collapse or erosion of the dome of a volcano

CATACLYSM: A violent change in the surface of the Earth

CAVE: A space underground of sufficient size that a person can enter, which has been naturally formed in a hillside or mountainous cliff

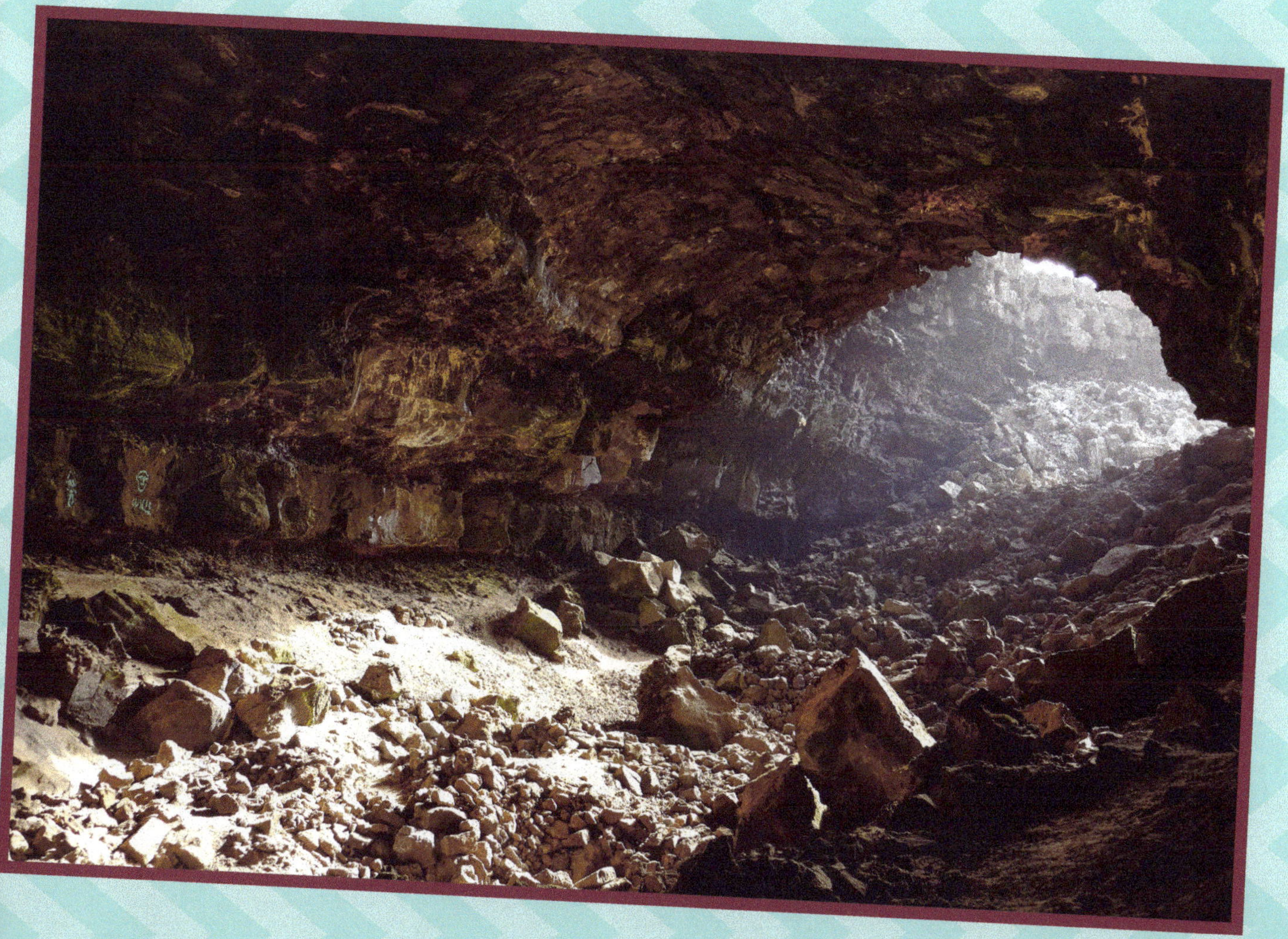

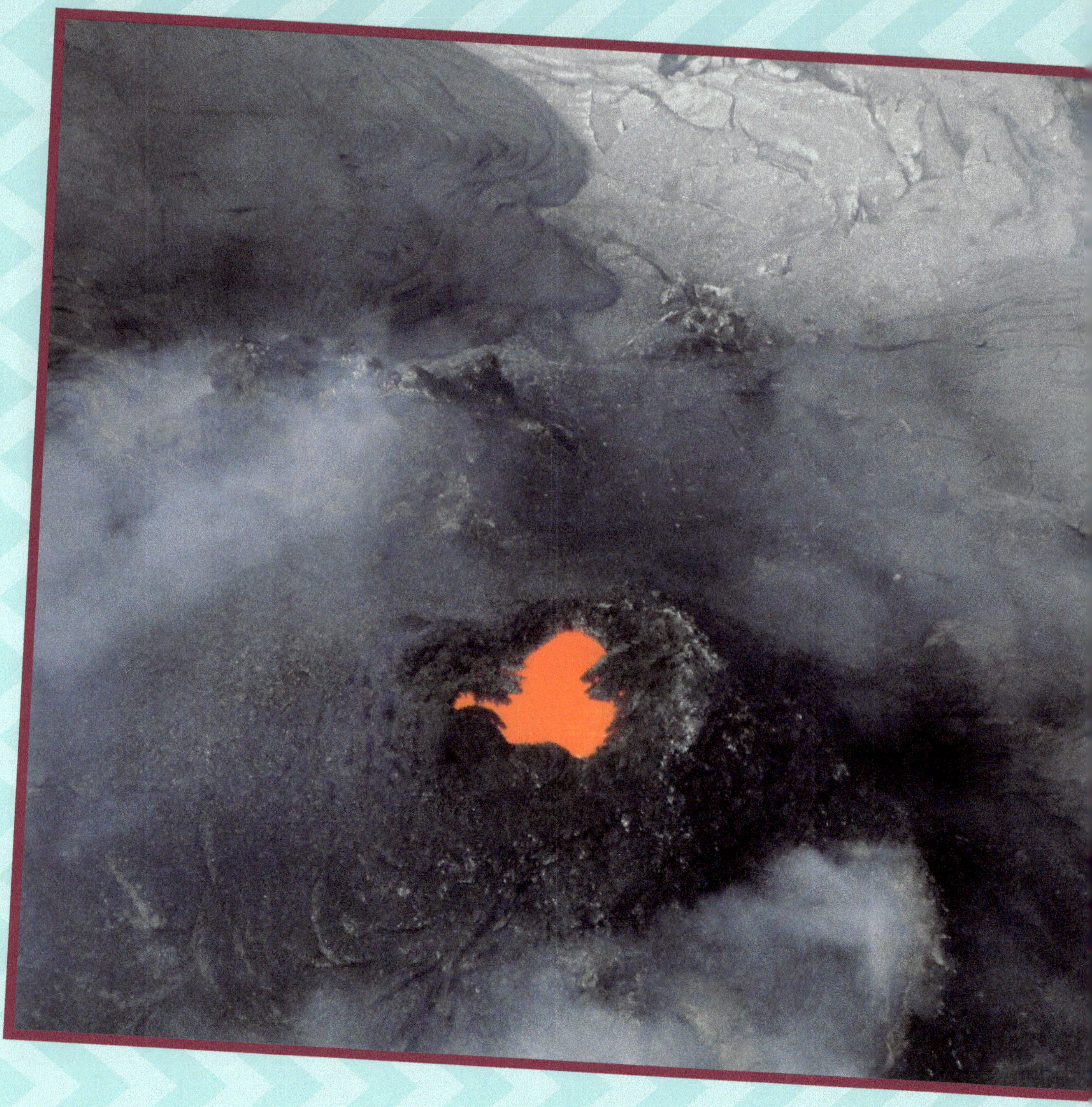

CENTRAL VENT: The most massive volcanic vent located at its cone-shaped center

CINDER CONE: A steep cone-shaped hill that's created around a volcanic vent

CLEAVAGE: The way a mineral's structure breaks into pieces when it is struck

CRYSTALLINE: Composed of crystals

CRYSTALS: Substances that are solid and that have a structure composed of geometric shapes

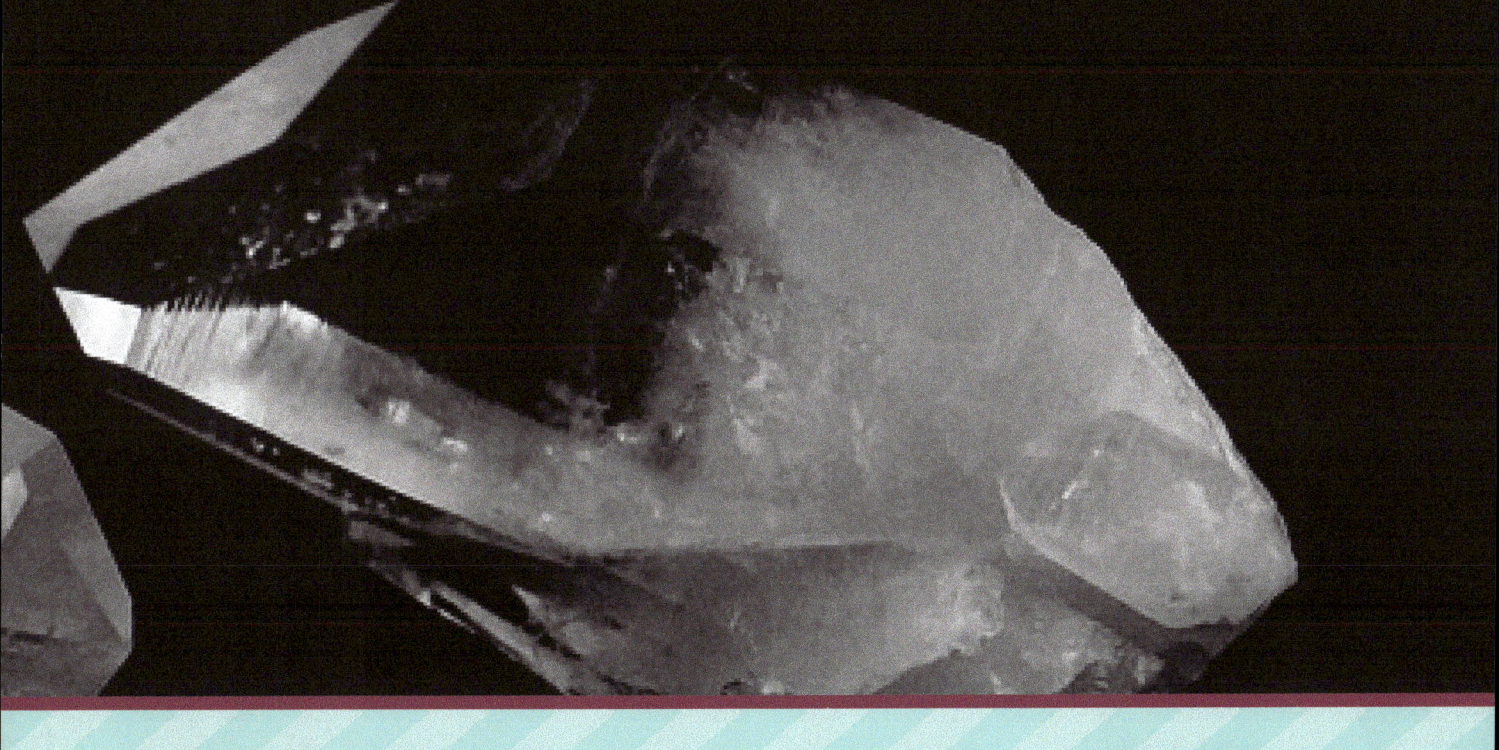

DELTA: The lowlands surrounding a river's mouth as it empties into another waterway

DOLOMITE: A type of sedimentary rock that is over 50% calcium-magnesium-carbonate, which is a mineral

DUNE: A sand mound that has been formed by either water or wind

EARTH'S CORE: The central region of the Earth, which is composed of intensely hot, solid matter primarily made up of iron as well as nickel

EARTH'S CRUST: Earth's outer surface layer, which is composed of rocks as well as minerals

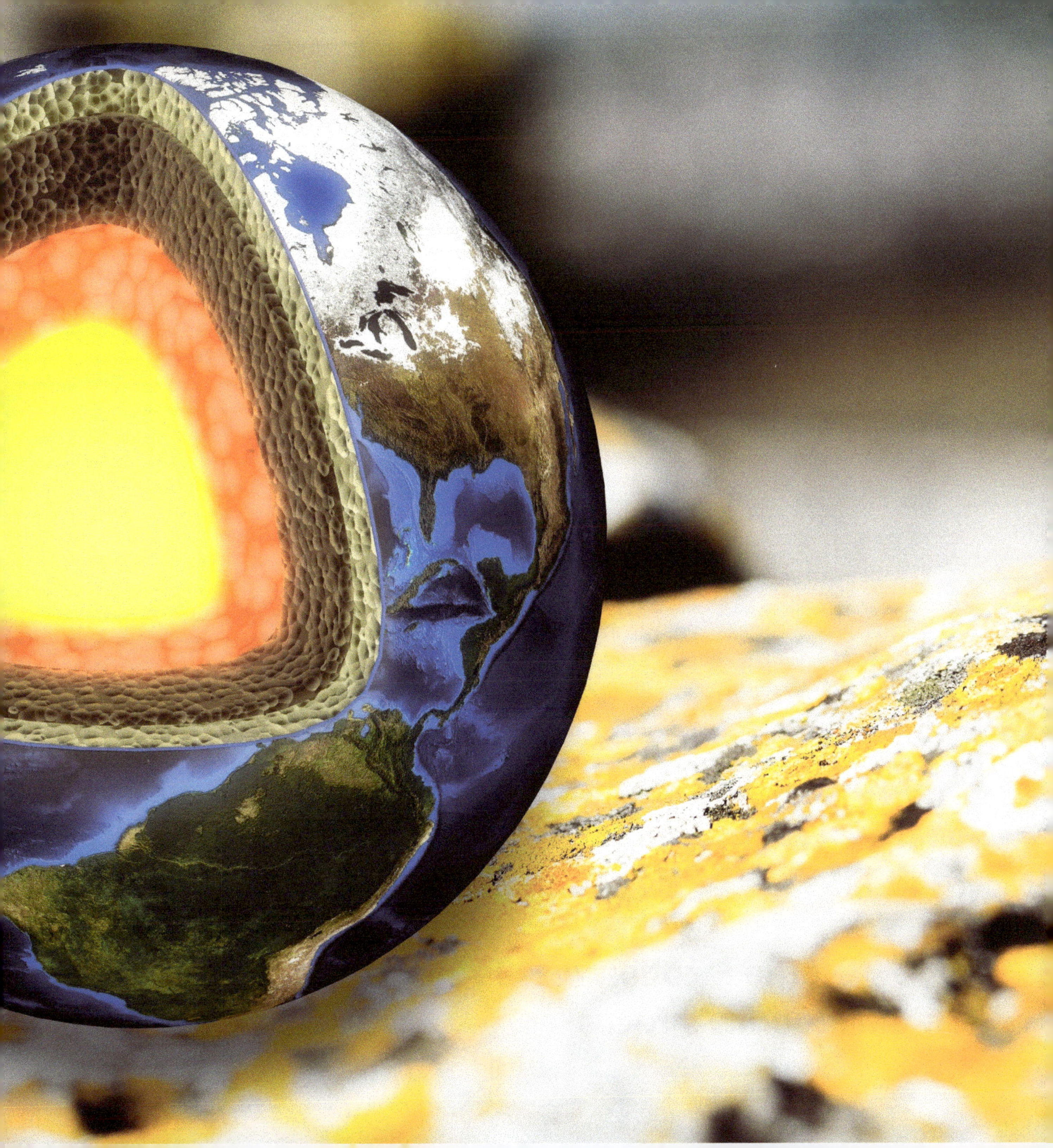

EARTHQUAKE: Shaking ground due to intense movement of the crust of the Earth and generally occurring at a fault line

EPICENTER: The location on the surface of the Earth above an earthquake's focus

EPOCH: A measure of time that is a part of a longer period of time and is divided into smaller distinct ages

EROSION: When the land's surface becomes weathered or loses material due to flowing water, high winds, or freezing ice

ESTUARY: A location where seawater and freshwater come together

EXTRUSIVE: Rocks that are created from the lava that flows from volcanoes

FAULT: A break in the layers of rocks in the crust of the Earth, where rocks on one side or the other have moved in relationship to each other

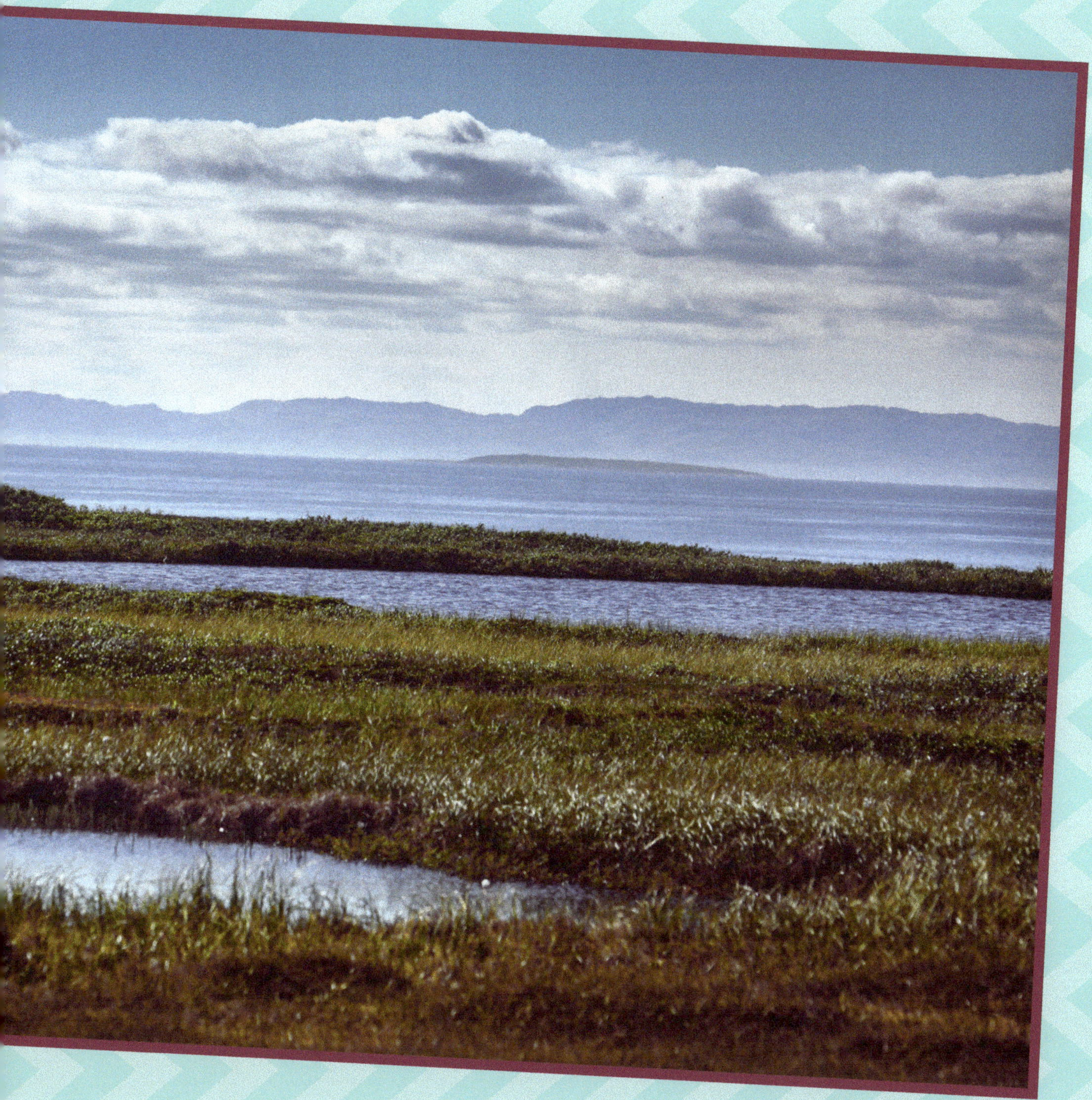

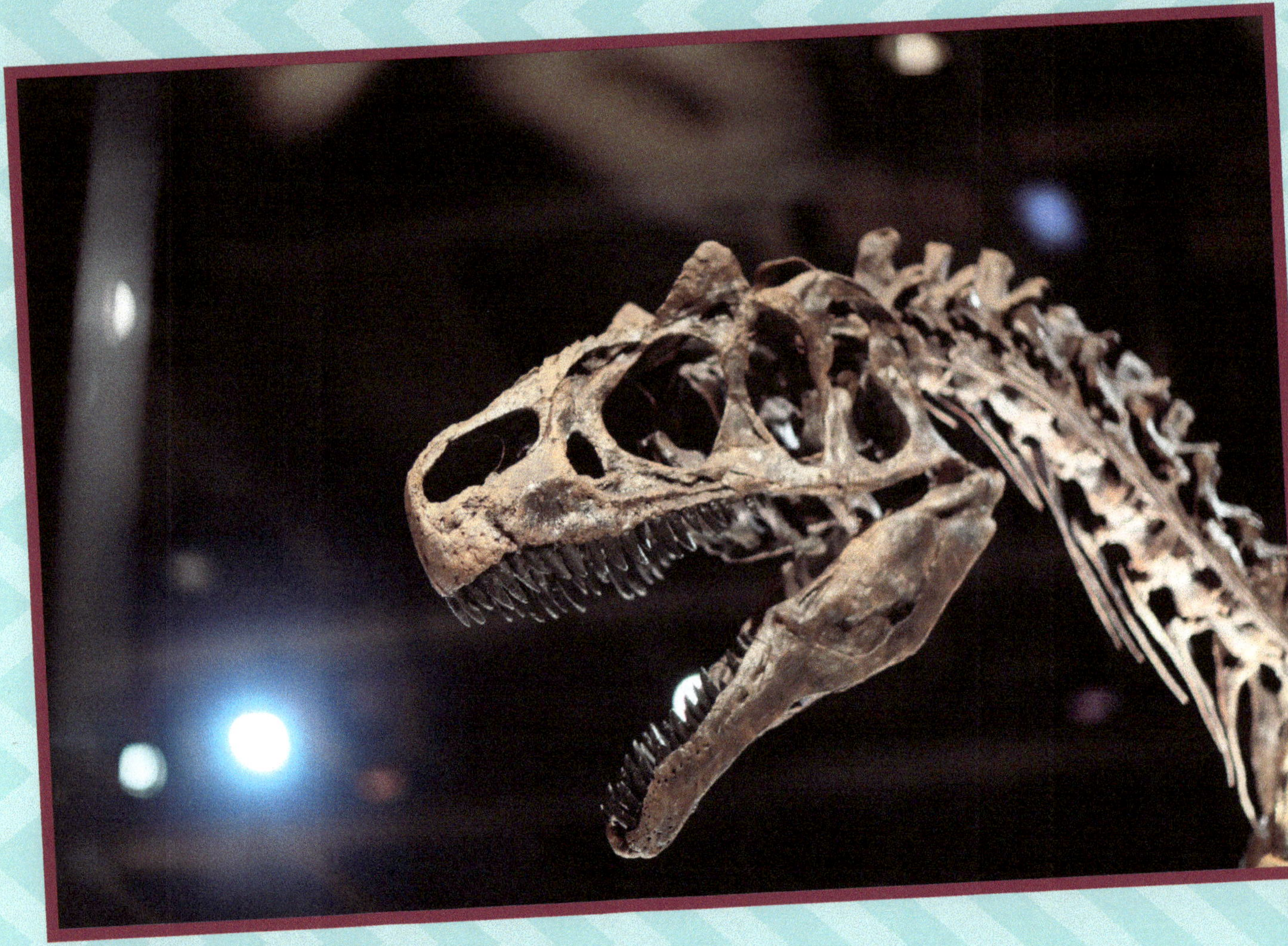

FIORD: A valley that once held a glacier but that now has a U-shape and is filled with water

FOCUS: The starting point within the Earth where an earthquake erupts, it's right below the earthquake's epicenter

FOSSIL: The remains of an animal or plant from prehistoric times that is preserved in rock

GEOLOGIST: A scientist who specializes in the field of geology

GEOLOGY: A field of study encompassing the Earth's structure, including its minerals and rocks as well as the forces that shape the Earth

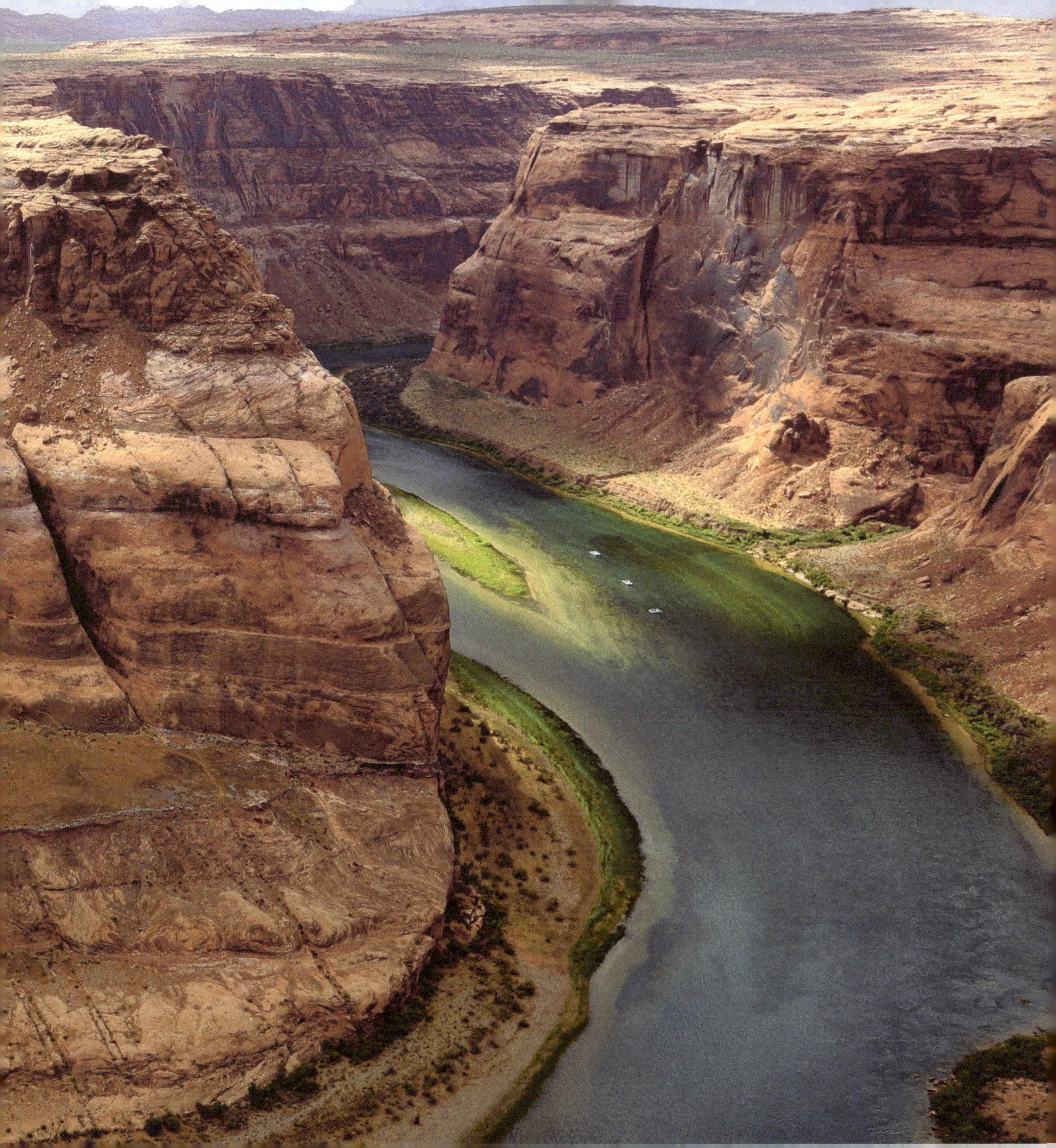

GEYSER: A hot, powerful spring of water that emits hot steam and water into the air

GLACIER: An enormous amount of ice that stays solid over a long time period

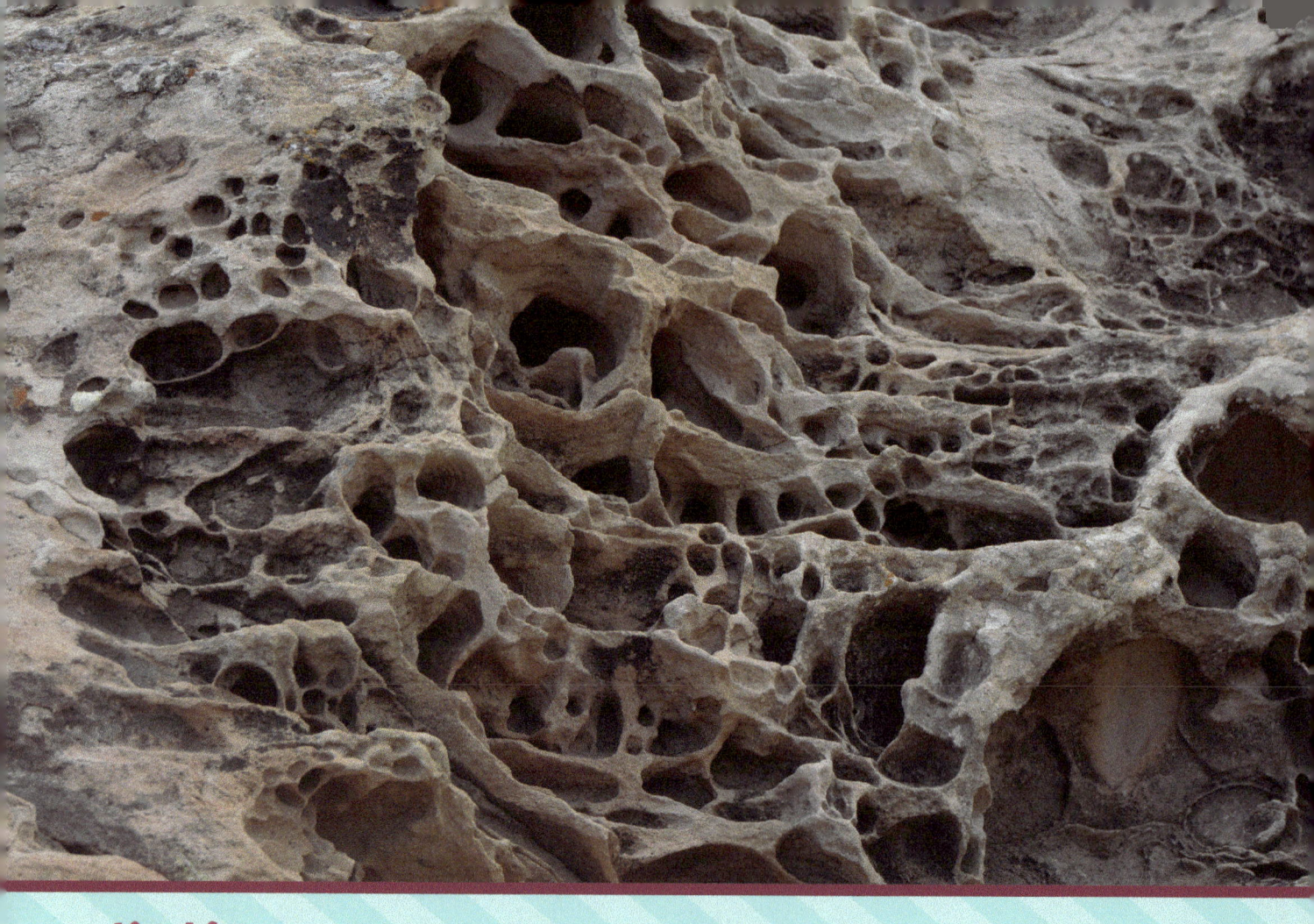

ICE AGE: Extremely cold spans of time in Earth's history when glaciers covered a large portion of the Earth's surface

IGNEOUS ROCK: A rock that has been formed by materials that were molten or partially molten

INTRUSIVE: Rocks that are created by magma when it solidifies under the Earth's surface

LAVA: Molten rock that has reached the surface of the Earth from volcanic activity

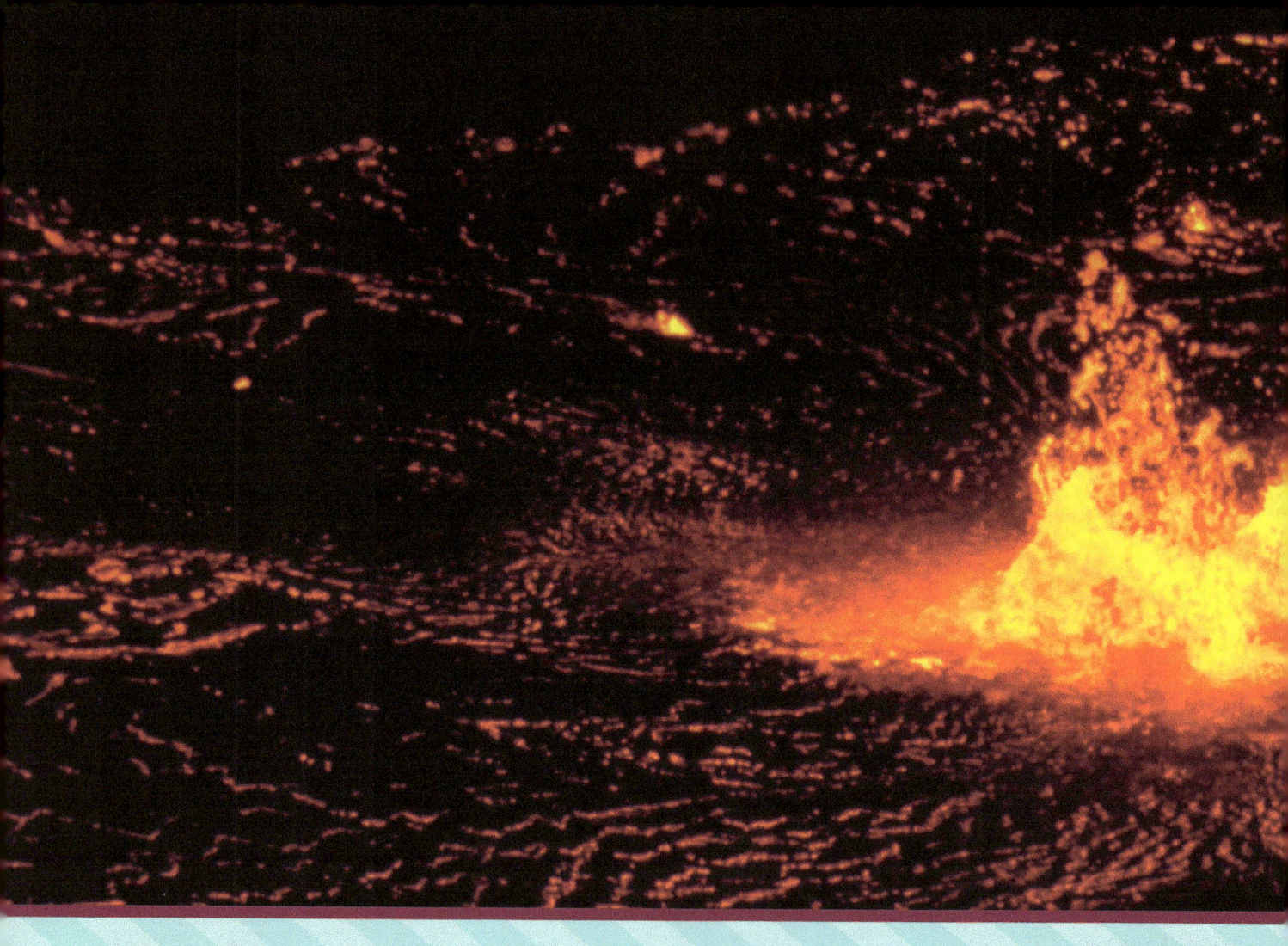

LIMESTONE: A type of sedimentary rock that is primarily composed of calcium carbonate in the form of calcite, which is a mineral

LUSTER: How a mineral's surface gives off light

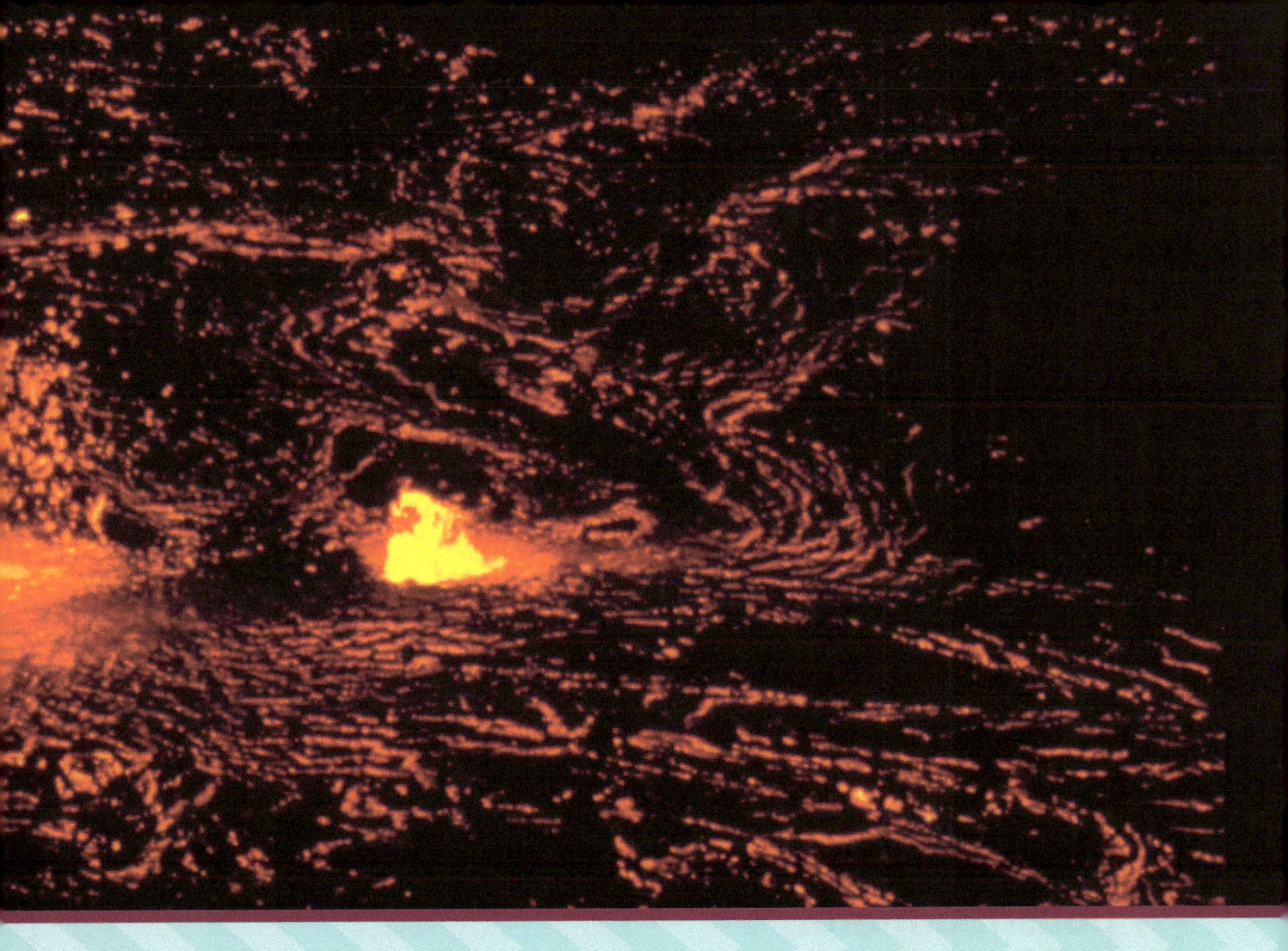

MAGMA: Hot, liquefied rock that is underneath the surface of the Earth--when it erupts from a volcano and flows on top of the Earth's surface, it's called lava

MAGNITUDE: A measure of the size of an earthquake

MANTLE: The interior section of the Earth that is located between its outer surface, which is called the crust, and its inner core

MESA: A formation of land that is not as extensive as a plateau, but is larger than a butte and has steep sides and a flattened top

METALLIC MINERAL: A mineral that looks similar to polished metal

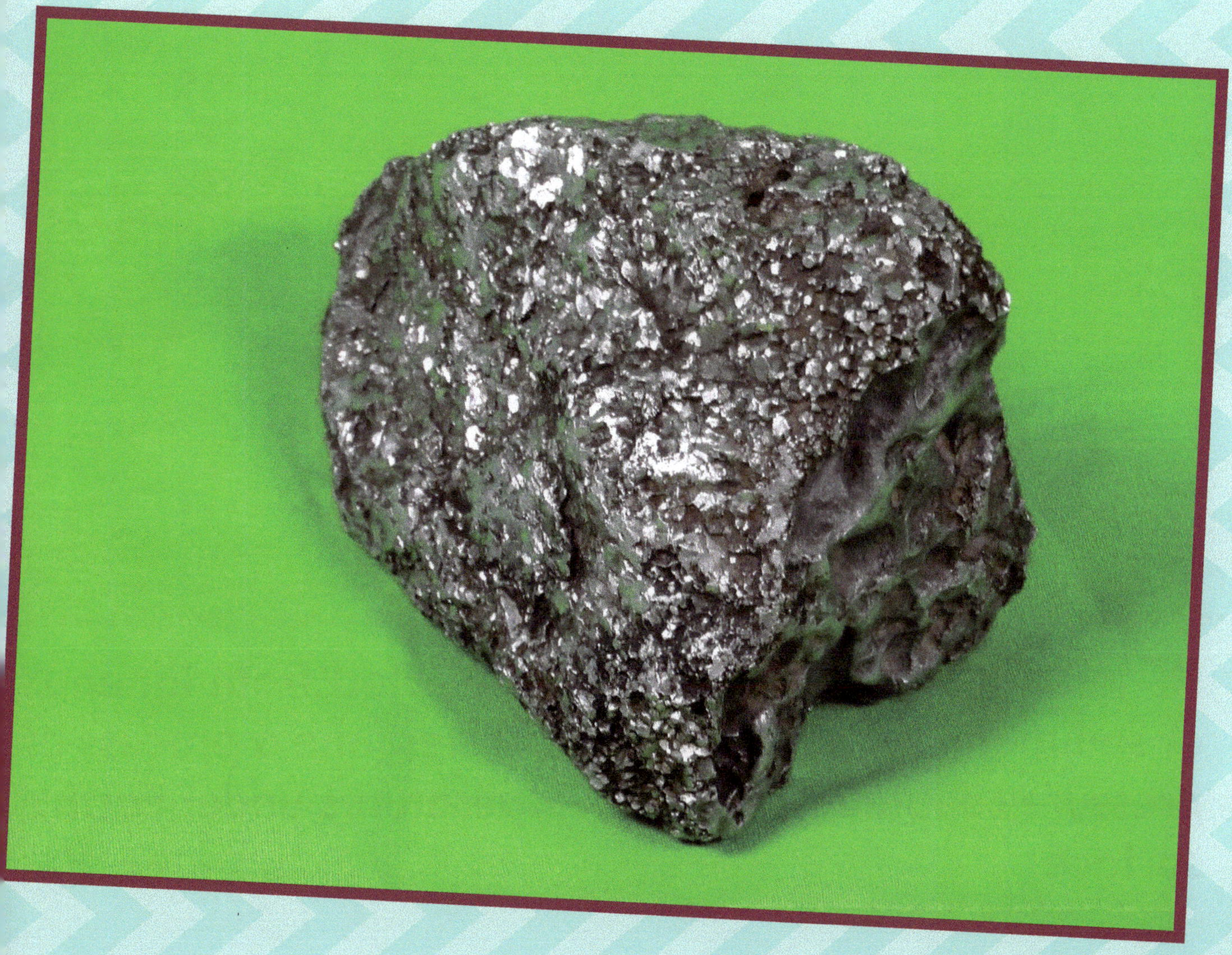

METAMORPHIC ROCK: A rock that is created from igneous or sedimentary rocks that have undergone a process of pressure coupled with high temperatures under Earth's surface

METEORITE: A stone that has traveled through space and penetrated Earth's atmosphere

MINERAL: A substance that is solid as well as inorganic and is formed by Earth's natural processes--it has a crystalline structure that can be described using chemical symbols

MOHS SCALE: A scale that describes a way to classify minerals based on their hardness

MOLTEN: Rocks and minerals in a liquid state due to intense heat

MOUNTAIN: A landform that rises up above the land that surrounds it, usually with a peak that is a minimum of 1,000 feet higher than sea level

OCEAN TIDE: The increase and decrease of coastline sea levels, which are influenced by the gravitational pull of the moon and the sun

PANGEA: A supercontinent that once joined all today's continents, which scientists believe was one enormous landmass over 300 million years in the past

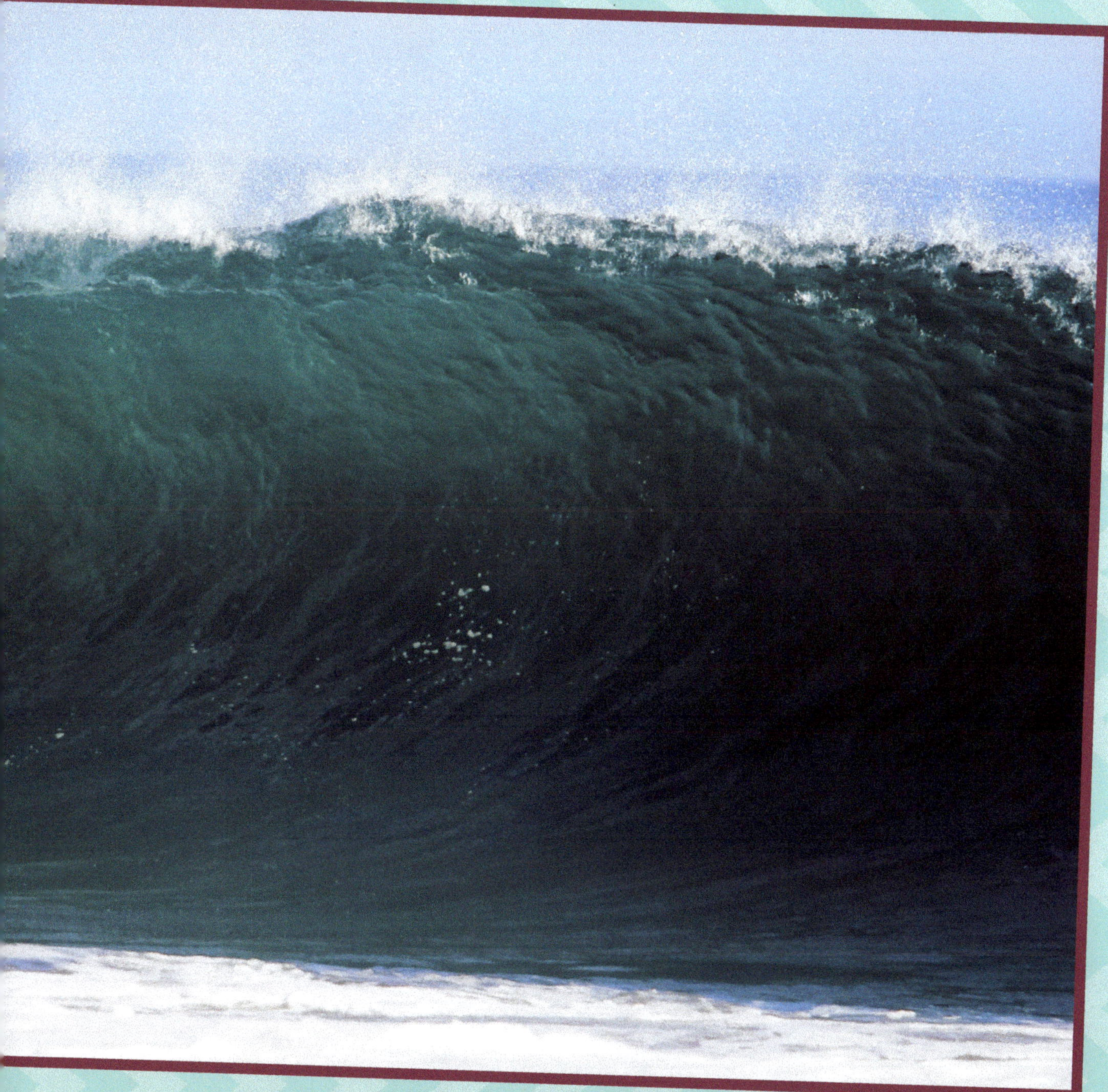

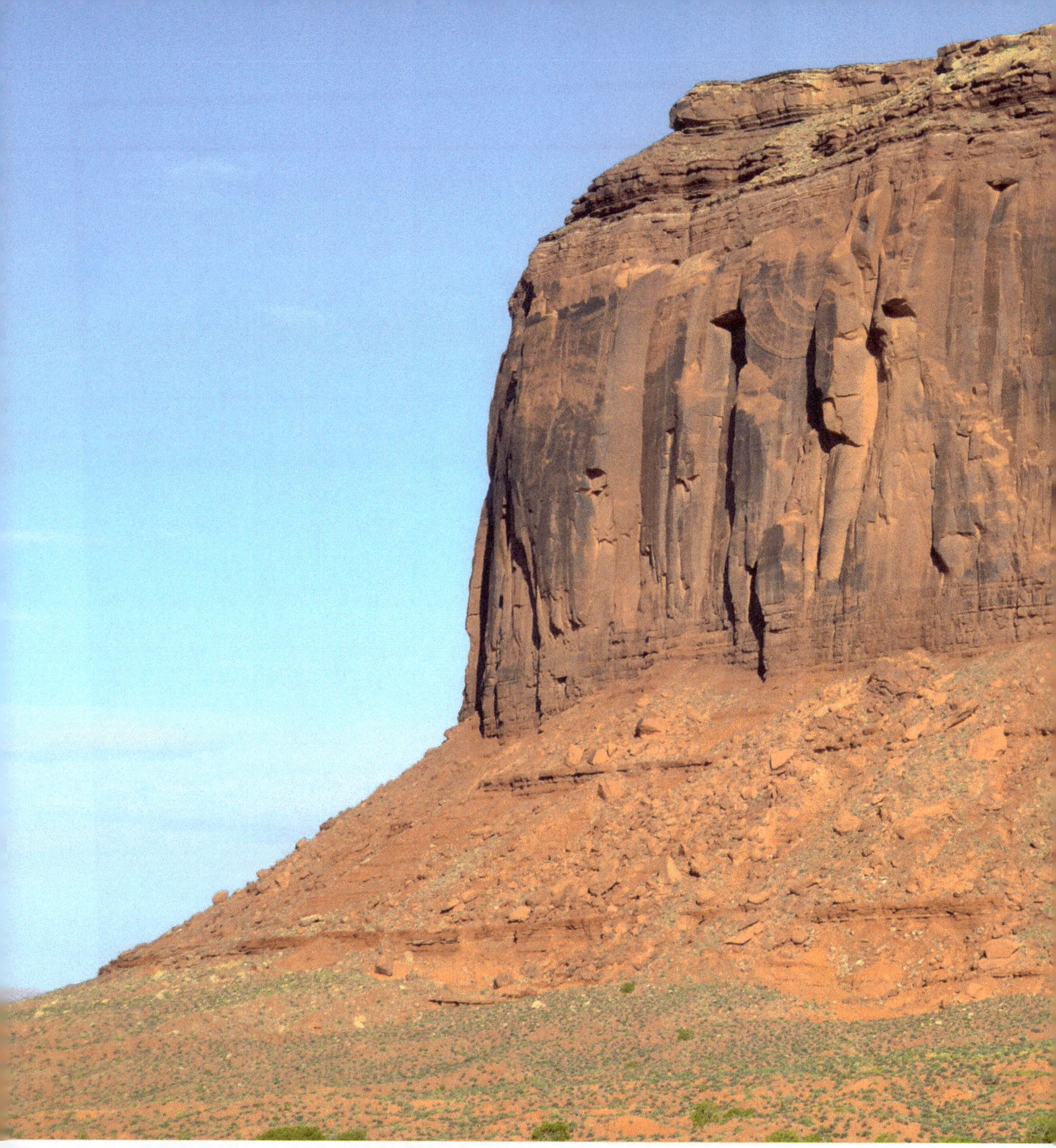

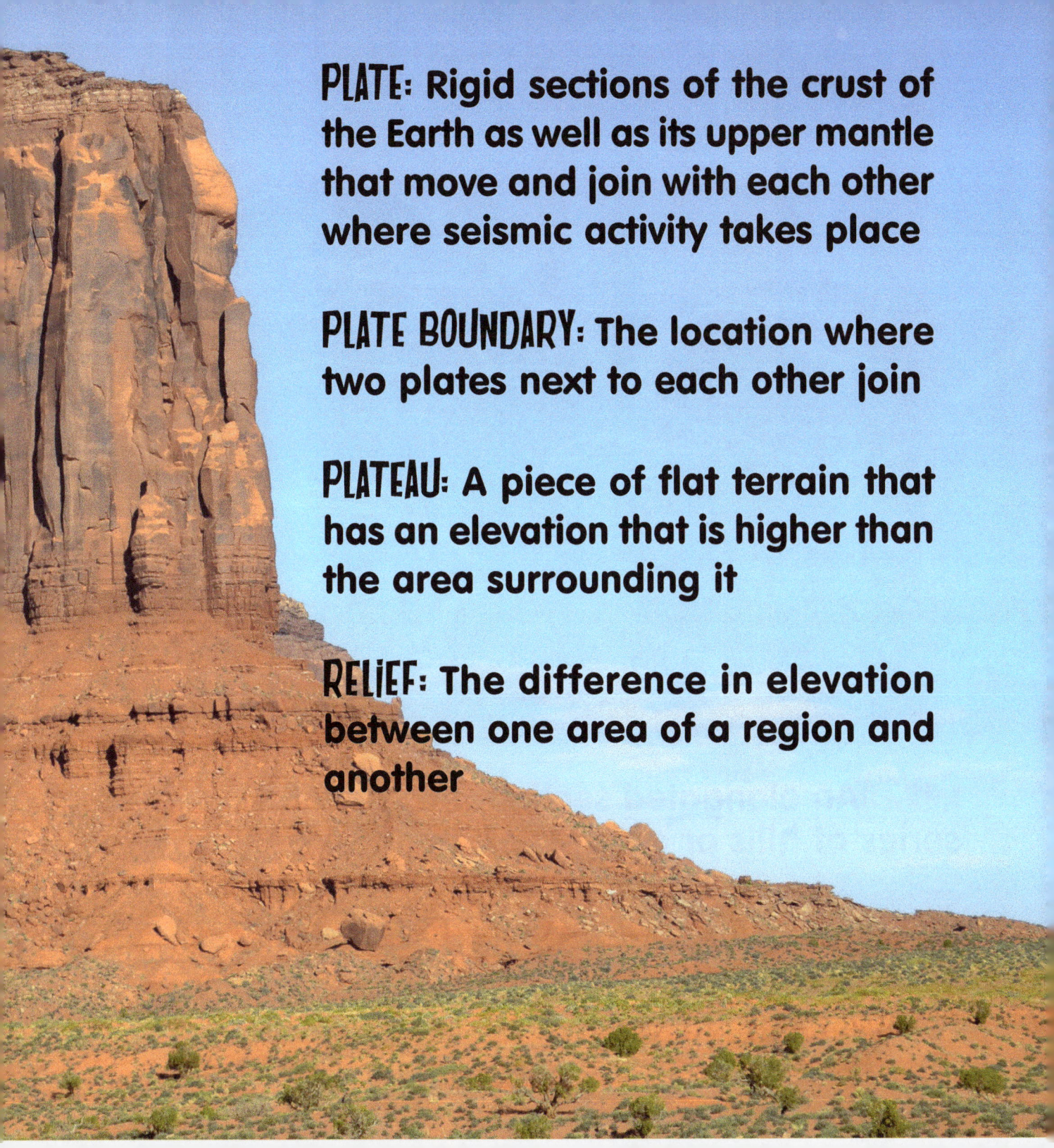

PLATE: Rigid sections of the crust of the Earth as well as its upper mantle that move and join with each other where seismic activity takes place

PLATE BOUNDARY: The location where two plates next to each other join

PLATEAU: A piece of flat terrain that has an elevation that is higher than the area surrounding it

RELIEF: The difference in elevation between one area of a region and another

RIDGE: An elongated section that traverses the top of a series of hills or a series of mountains

RIFT: A location where the crust of the Earth is being separated

ROCK: A substance that is solid and is composed of a number of different minerals and sometimes fossils or organic material

ROCK CYCLE: The stages where rock transforms into different forms

SEDIMENT: Fragments of rock that combine with mud and sand and fall to the bottom of the sea or other waterway

SEDIMENTARY ROCK: Rocks that are formed when loose sediment becomes compacted and hardened over long periods of time

SEISMIC ACTIVITY: Ground vibration that is due to the release of energy from rocks that are breaking, generally caused by the movement of tectonic plates

SOIL: The top layer of Earth's surface that contains dirt and organic material and where plants take root

SOLIDIFY: When a molten liquid, such as magma, changes to a solid

STRATA: The layers formed by sedimentary rock

STREAK TEST: A test that geologists and mineralogists use to classify a mineral based on the color of its streak

TECTONIC PLATES: Enormous regions of the crust of the Earth, which move slowly underneath and on top of one another

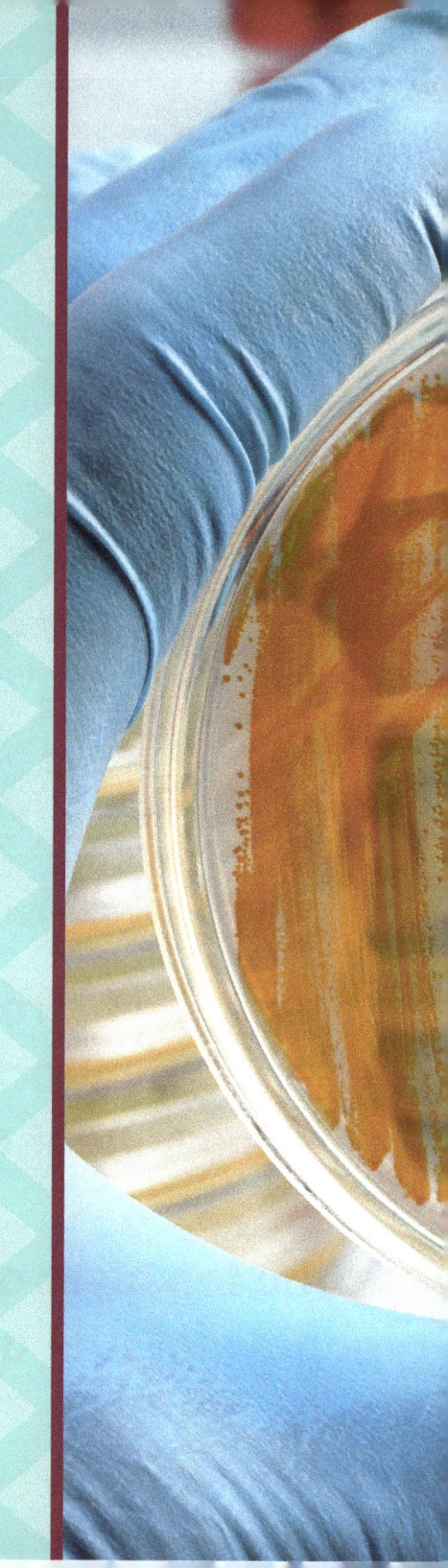

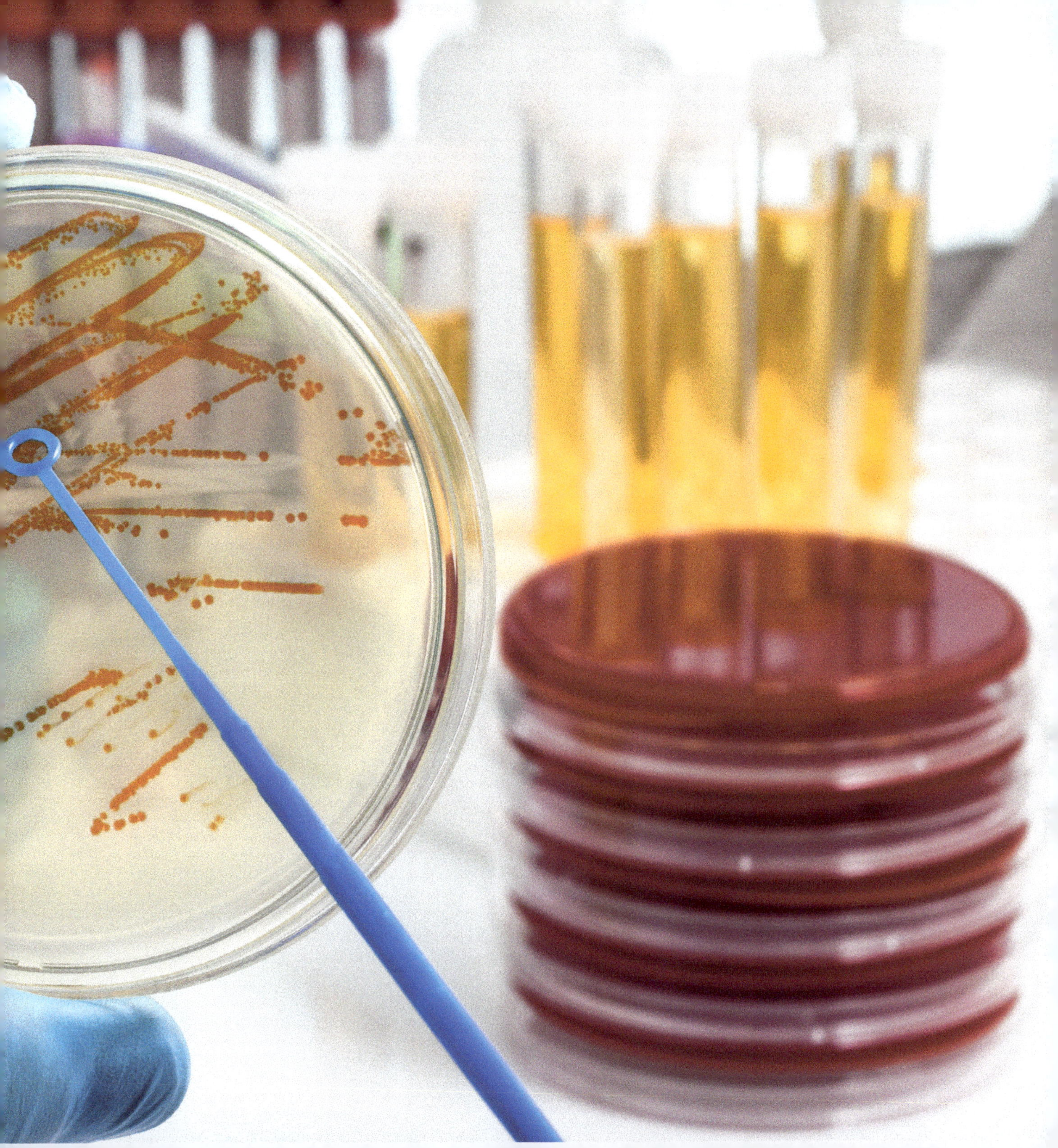

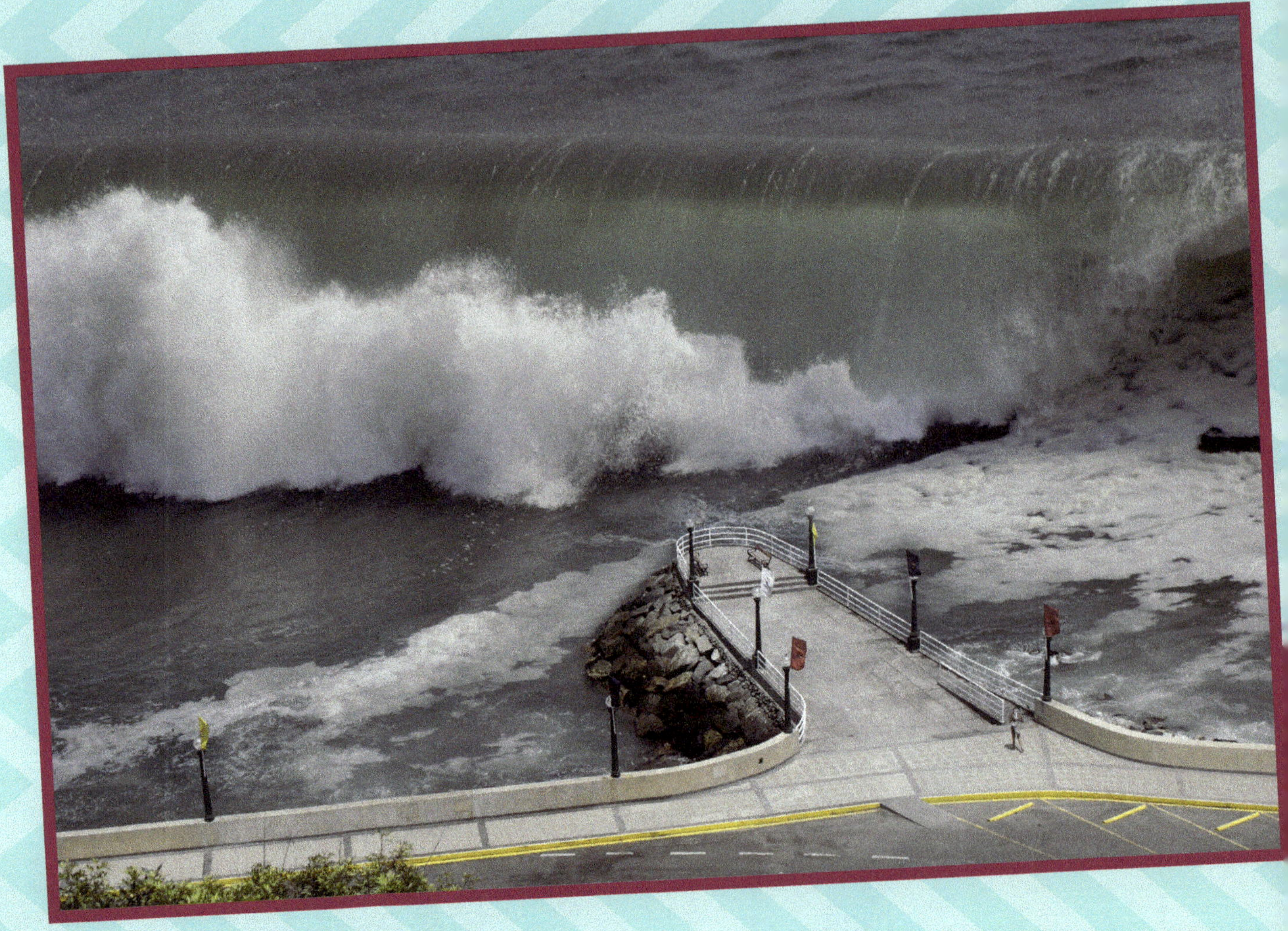

TOPOGRAPHY: The physical characteristics of a region of land

TSUNAMI: An enormous wave that is caused by earthquake and causes coastline destruction

VOLCANO: A crack in the crust of the Earth where magma erupts and comes to the surface as lava

WEATHERING: The gradual wearing away of rock that is exposed to extremes in temperature, wind, and water

WHAT THE EARTH IS MADE OF

Once you read and study the terms in this Pictionary, you'll be able to better understand the materials the Earth is made of and the forces that shape the Earth. Perhaps someday you'll study to become a geologist. Geologists are scientists who study rocks and minerals as well as landforms and the forces that shape them.

Awesome! Now that you've read about geology terms you may want to read about rocks and minerals in the Baby Professor book *Little Rocks & Small Minerals!*

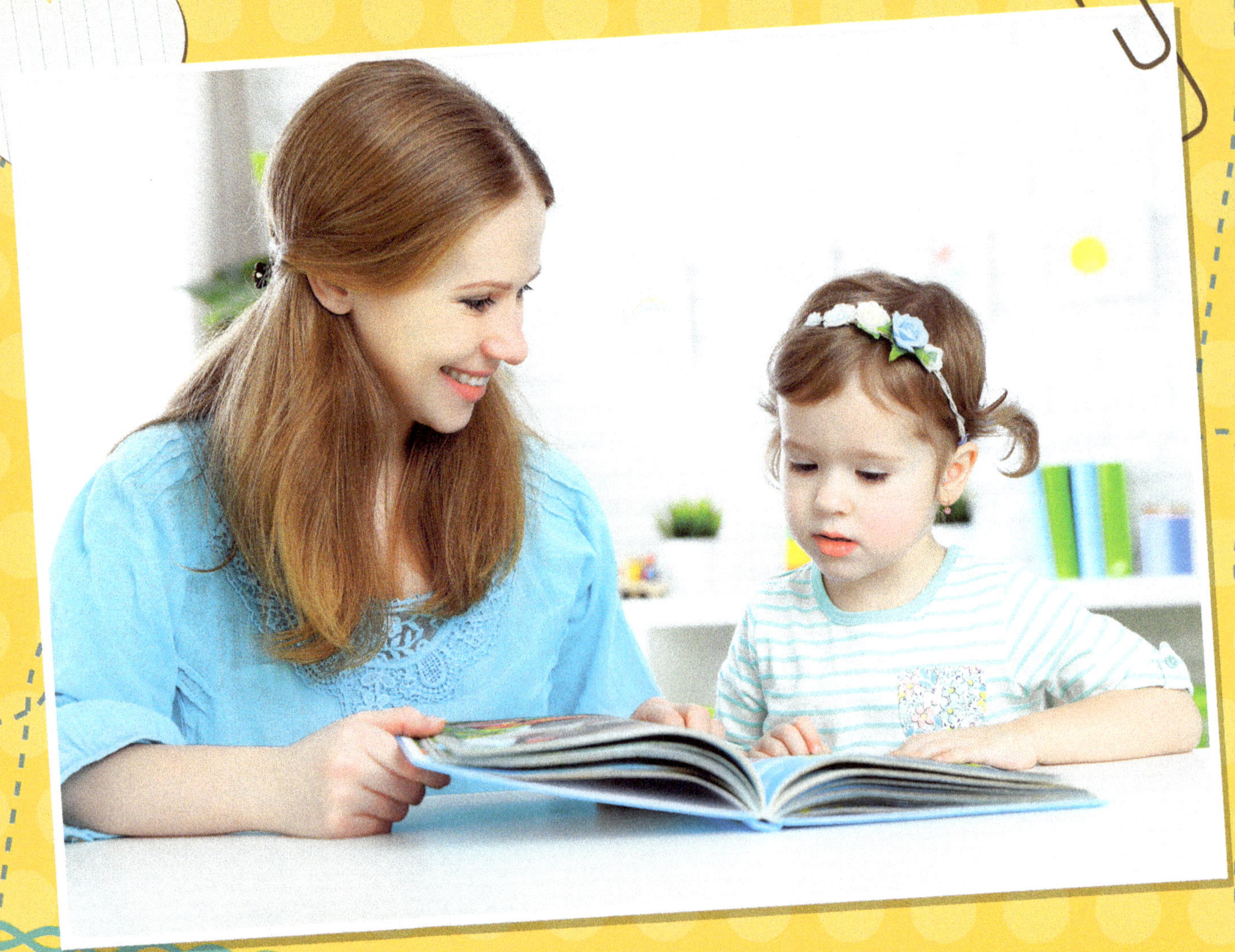

Visit

BABY PROFESSOR
EDUCATION KIDS

www.BabyProfessorBooks.com

to download Free Baby Professor eBooks
and view our catalog of new and exciting
Children's Books

Lightning Source UK Ltd.
Milton Keynes UK
UKHW051920011121
393220UK00005B/83